M000301463

HOW TO
MONETIZE DESPAIR

Poems

LISA MOTTOLO

HOW TO MONETIZE DESPAIR
Copyright © 2023 Lisa Mottolo
All Rights Reserved.
Published by Unsolicited Press.
Printed in the United States of America.
First Edition.

No part of this book may be used or reproduced in any manner
whatsoever without written permission except in the case of brief
quotations embodied in critical articles or reviews.

Attention schools and businesses: for discounted copies on large
orders, please contact the publisher directly.

For information contact:
Unsolicited Press
Portland, Oregon
www.unsolicitedpress.com
orders@unsolicitedpress.com
619-354-8005

Front Cover Design: Lisa Mottolo
Editor: S.R. Stewart

ISBN: 978-1-956692-78-5

For you in particular

Contents

PART II: HOW TO REMOVE THE KETTLE FROM THE FLAME RIGHT BEFORE ITS HIDEOUS WHISTLE

Acknowledgements

How to Write About Trauma, Penn Review.

Your Mother Gave Birth to You, Louisiana Literature.

The No Excuse Exercise Guide, Ethel Zine.

Balloon and *Breadbox*, Slipstream.

I keep talking about my dead mother, like a farm that never forgets a drought, SWWIM.

My Mother Drank Black Coffee, Stonecoast Review.

A Philosopher Afraid of the News, Santa Clara Review.

Stephen Hawking and Robotic Dolls, Diagram.

The Vacant Expression of a Cell Phone Screen, The Laurel Review.

The New Yorker and *The Electric City*, Albany Poets.

Part I:

How to Be a Flock of Burning Canaries

How to Write About Trauma

It is so peaceful to be unconscious.
The EMT cradled me like a long sleep

as he carefully pulled me from the wreckage.
My mother was in the front seat.

Not unconscious, just dead.
A different, permanent type of peacefulness.

I'm taking a free course, now.
How to write about trauma.

All the students are women,
and I wonder if they're more prone to trauma

or if it's because the trauma is often the result of men.
I'm not saying it is, I'm just wondering if it is.

My mother was driving us home from her fiancé's house
after a long day and she fell asleep at the wheel.

Everyone always encouraged me to feel guilty.
"Maybe you could have woken her before you crashed."

I don't know, because I don't remember.
My brain won't let me remember,

and that's probably for the best.
All I remember is seeing and feeling blackness,

like a starless space,
and hearing my mother's last words,

"what time do you think we'll be home?"

The Loneliest Blue is the Reflection of the Sky

God is the expectations of our ancestors, and I come from a family with low expectations. Upstairs, the carpet is half-removed and folded over, and my blood from two decades ago is a dry splash in the corner. My father slowly paces in the kitchen. He picks up crumbs I can't see and rants about mice. I ask him if his eyes are blue or green, and he says, "I don't pay attention to that shit." I remember putting pink barrettes in his curly mullet as a child. I probably knew his irises then, in the way I know the sunlight while actively avoiding looking at the sun. The walls of his house are quiet. I chew my water. I eat with the mouth of an unanswered question. I want to tell him I once thought I'd catch bubbles of silence in my mouth until life ended. That I was once washed with grief until I was clean as used soap. He tells me to I need to go to church. But my friend and I both read the Bible and The God Delusion together, and we came out dumber with each book. Now I only read poetry, and who knows how that is affecting my brain. But more importantly, who knows the burning last spatter of feces from birds that come barreling out of the sky when a father doesn't respond to "I love you"? I take a bath and it feels like cold wind. I listen to the clouds, and the edges crisp like the ends of cigarettes. I have found the edges of my father's voice. They hang like frayed strings longing for ties. I've almost found a way to harness the stringy clouds. I've almost found a way to strangle the sky.

There are Monsters

I once killed several caterpillars
below a tree that was dripping with them

as though they were rain or sap,
and their falls were silent as a balloon.

Don't ask me about their faces,
too small to know there are monsters

they have evolved to evade.
Really, the tree was dripping.

All I ever wanted was to marry the Titanic.
To break into gigantic pieces

so everyone would know
something happened here.

But instead I became a daughter left
by a mother who loved lighthouses,

those romantic things with bright lights
that show the ship the shore.

Don't Forget to Take Your Heart Medicine

Everything is possible. I am capable. We can seek help from a god we don't believe exists. I am only bad at things because I believe I am bad at them. Etc. etc. etc. Just one time I'd like to open a self-help book and see a picture of the author at their absolute worst, and have them say, "I know what you're thinking. What a before picture! But this was this morning." Or perhaps it could have a photograph of an old, lonely man covered in liver spots, looking out a window as a recreational activity even though there's a brick wall blocking any view, and the place beside the window is the coldest spot in the house, and it is winter in Chicago, and the man is nursing a hemorrhoid, and by nursing I simply mean he has a donut cushion, not anything crazy, and there's no pictures on the wall, unless you count the note beside the bathroom mirror that says, "don't forget to take your heart medicine," and somehow you can tell all of these from the photograph, and the caption simply says, "This is your future even if you try."

Your Mother Gave Birth to You

and you were a tiny button that rolled soundlessly
underneath the hospital cabinet.

Soundless, like the brushing of unsnarled hair.

Now, it's the first day of the rest of your life,
or so say the inspirational memes,

and one wonders if such a thing is diminished
by so many insisting upon it.

But you're trying, regardless.

You're dying your hair dark to look less basic.
You're bleaching your hair light to look less basic.

You've thrown away a pair of shorts
you've accepted you'll never fit into again.

But you still have anxiety dreams about public restrooms
with unsatisfactory privacy

and not being able to find a classroom
when it's been ages since that was relevant,

And you want to hear about the time I killed a mouse
and told its dead body how sorry I was.

I can tell you that I don't remember its fuzzy face,
as its insides became outsides

and something new was born:
a wet display of death that seemed to breathe.

I can tell you that I was terrified the only difference
between being dead and live

is a tired heart just tapping along like a workaholic's
fingertips upon a keyboard.

I can tell you I was remembering that apple seeds
contain arsenic.

I was remembering that many think the worst thing
about breast cancer is a possible mastectomy,

when it's actually death.

The No Excuse Exercise Guide

There was a book published in the 70s called the *No Excuse Exercise Guide*. It was pink and purple and there was a copy on my grandma's liquor shelf. I read it a few times, as I didn't find my grandpa's Tom Clancy novels appealing. My grandma told me feeling fat is the worst feeling in the world. She was once a person buying, and carrying home, and flipping through that book. She spent years preparing her body to ultimately be viewed in a coffin, only for there to not be a service. And who knows why? Money? Distance? What matters is that it didn't happen. She did crossword puzzles every morning on newspapers that are no longer in circulation and had piles of reading material on preventing Alzheimer's. She didn't want to end up like her mother. But she did. I think the advice offered to prevent disease is just there to take up space in media and act as another page on which to insert an advertisement. But that seems to be virtually everything – a person thinking "what will fill space?" and there was my grandma, saying "filling space is the worst feeling in the world."

The Hummingbird's Displays

A ruby-throated hummingbird came up to the window
and I missed it because I was reading a poem about God.

It caught my eye as it flew away,
its crimson neck like a ball of lightning

exacting revenge for some avian cultural issue
humans will never understand.

This is my life now,
missing one beautiful thing

because I'm transfixed by another,
and some people would say this is disgusting.

"Whenever there is an opportunity, you just sit there,"
my grandma to me said after my mom died.

I ask myself what opportunity is offered
by the disintegration of a mother's sacred soul.

Oh! An iridescent flicker of wing!
I missed another of the hummingbird's displays.

Someday this beautiful thing will die, and no human will
see
its body because wild animals know to crawl away

and hide as they become weak.
We, on the other hand, shake our leaky wounds

in the spotlight, saying "save me, save me,"
and I wonder what my grandma would think of that

and I wonder if she was right
and I wonder if she was right about me.

Obituary for a Small Parrot

I drove home from the vet with her body in a cardboard
box, and the trees marched past with stiff brown coats,

some demanding I scrape a thick string of blood from my
heart

and present it as an explanation for my neglect.
I didn't have a shovel, or a place to dig, or the energy to dig,

or the energy to buy a shovel,
so the box became increasingly caked in frost

in my freezer over the course of a year,
the seasons moving through like laughter of past children,

feet shaking the apartment floors with a grating glee.

It had been good, nothing but good,
but life was back to a sputtering hose

in the winter, the visible breath of a woodland animal,
the idea of a never-ending universe surrounding these things

and compressing them
until they were less notable than a leaking can of crushed
tomatoes.

Write About Death

It is fortunate
death is soft like mushroom
or a bruised bone,
because this allows us to handle it
without callusing our hands.
I am tired of things that sit in my hands
too lightly or even too beautifully,
and this is why I don't write about death
as often as I used to.
I clasp every death I've ever known
into my palms like a locket
that closes too tightly
and I keep them there
as though I value a tragedy
that hangs around the neck
pretty.

I keep talking about my dead mother, like a farm that never forgets a drought

And by "talking," I mean remembering the time I worked as a cashier at a little Italian supermarket and a blonde-haired woman asked, "what does your mother think of your piercings?" and I told her she was dead and she laughed like Fran Drescher.

And by "remembering the time I worked as a cashier," I mean delicately folding the memory like an easily wrinkled shirt and placing it on the top shelf in my closet, where I can see it each time I get dressed.

And by "delicately folding the memory," I mean letting it sink into my gums like the taste of blood. Like the taste of flossing after going through a depressive slump where you didn't floss at all and now you probably have gum disease.

And by "letting it sink into my gums," I mean putting it on a plate straight from the farm that never forgets a drought, and dissecting it with knife and fork like I have a child mouth that can only handle small bites.

We Only Speak Well of the Dead

My mother was a pond of shade,
a green and grey, like the blur of a chalkboard

to a kid without glasses.
She knew the big cows we saw on trips

I did not actually see.
She knew I pushed my face up against the car window,

trying to read the street signs.
My nerves grow into flaming streaks of yellow

like I am a flock of burning canaries
when I think of everything I was supposed to learn

and didn't, but I can't tell you this story
because we only speak well of the dead.

Balloon

This is me trying to describe the expression that I never saw
on my mother's face until she was in a coffin;

the expression that says, "my mouth is wired shut so it
doesn't hang open as you look at me."

She laid helpless as they sewed wire through her gums,
 her skin slack and bunching around their hands.

It made a sound like a needle running
through an airless balloon.

And I'm sorry but it just doesn't look right
the way her mouth is closed.

If you tried to make her look like she was sleeping
I'll have you know

that you just made her look like she was dead.
I didn't know about the embalming process when I was 14.

Maybe I was just stupid.
I didn't know that at the wake she would be missing

all of her organs,
that she would be a shell like a Russian nesting doll
I'm just trying to explain how horrible going to your
mother's funeral is,

not trying to bother you.
My grandfather's wife asked, "does that look like your
mommy?"

with a smile. I said "no," because it did not,
because my mom never looked dead before.

She responded by just smiling bigger,
and I still don't understand what the fuck that was about.

Immune and Joyful Children

When we travelled south, the billboards would say *hell is real*, and the fruit snack packages would say *made with real sugar*. "Apparently, a standard for quality, for hell and for sugar," we told our stuffed animals, "is the mere fact of its realness." I don't remember a young hurt like the one before and after a birthday party, where I would reach for a slice of pastel cake I didn't want (I just knew I was supposed to want it) and I wanted for presents that I knew wouldn't fulfill me (but would sit on my bedroom floor like a log burned through). We're all assumed to have been immune and joyful children: Immune to the depressive qualities of quickly tiring toys, and immune to the disappointment of waiting for summer all year long, just for summer to be a more boring and more hot type of sadness. When we travelled south, the billboards would say *hell is real*. And even as children, we would say "that is silly." But we would also wonder.

White Plates

My friend said
"I can't forgive myself
for my miscarriage"
as she cut up sandwiches
for her kids,
first into triangles,
then into even smaller triangles,
then into shapeless pieces,
with jelly rolling out from between
the bits of bread,
plopping into pink clumps
on the white plates
like newborn
mice.

My Mother Drank Black Coffee

My mother drank black coffee. It swung her through the day like an ax with a loose head. Her fingers, sensitive twigs, wrapped around the handle of a mug. A mug that at some point after she died was taken to a dump in New York, then to the ocean, where it attached itself to a sea creature's head, blocking its sharp lips, there to remain until the creature starved and crumbled into the wet sand.

/

Do you also feel nostalgic when you see a woman dressed in all black? Perhaps it is what we hope for. Each day we carry the limp bodies of genuine laughter but we can count the funerals on one hand. When do I wear my black dress for the stiff birds that once spoke outside my window?

/

I feel my throat swell when thinking of throwing away some broken plastic thing I have stuffed in my closet. A garbage truck driver, his words an expanding puff of dirt and vinegar chips, told me recycled items are used to make layers between trash at the dump. I don't know if that's true but I am sad.

/

My mother doesn't drink black coffee, anymore. She drinks what is brewed from the grounds of the cemetery and it pulls her through the spacious night like a whale's closing jaw. Her fingers are still wrapped around each other as the funeral home employees placed them, resting over her stomach which is now just a dusty spine.

/

I would like if we could return to burying the dead with their possessions. Not because we believe in an afterlife of people but because we know the afterlife of garbage. How it sits in piles of shredded tires and the blood of plastic.

/

Next time I break a coffee mug, I will go back to New York and bury it with my mother. I will situate some sensitive looking twigs into a cross. And I will feel that I have done something, but I will have done nothing at all.

Part II:

How to Remove the Kettle from the Flame
Right Before its Hideous Whistle

A Philosopher Afraid of the News

Wait for me in the sink.
Wait for me in the mirror.
Wait for me on the bathroom floor.
Good, the cockroach has followed my orders.
Now remind me with the weakness of your exoskeleton
that we are all expendable.
He touches his antenna to the wall.
You're right. The wall is weak. It cannot even contain
voices. Voices, of all delicate things!
He touches his prickly brown leg to a crack in the tile.
Yes, scientists still are unsure what lies beneath the
earth's crust, and that gives validity to the idea of hell.
His antennas raise sharply.
It's true! Haven't you seen the news?
I turn on the sun lamp. He runs to hide behind
the garbage can, his feet going back and forth along
the floor like windshield wipers
Ah, how predictable, a philosopher afraid
of the news.
I pick up the garbage can. He sits still.
Why display your weakness then attempt to resist death?
He sits still.
Oh, what a display.

I smoosh him with a wad of toilet paper. I flush it all down the toilet. I stare at the lid.

God, please protect us from these things.

The Vacant Expression of a Cell Phone Screen

Bird bones are hollow to make it easier for them to fly,
and I think about this a lot

when I look at the vacant expression of a cellphone screen

because achieving a reduced stress level may require some
shallow activities.

We will argue with ourselves ad nauseum over the reason
to use and not use our devices

and our arguments are pitched like a fork against a glass

they bring attention, they hurt the ears, but we listen
in the hopes of a reasonable philosophy

or a study from a reputable news source.

I'm still waiting for the moment where I'm taken aside
to be told something important

but it could be that I am the one who will be taking others
aside and telling them those things

and how lonely to be assigned that task
considering that my social anxiety will keep me from doing
it

so I will be clutching to the information

and typing and retyping it in my phone's note app

wondering if any brave person has experienced this amount
of hesitance

and asking myself if phones keep getting lighter

so they are easier to attach to our existences

like a bird's bones are hollow to make it easier for them to
fly

Commercials

The old woman is working on some little projects. Projects like how to remove the kettle from the flame right before its hideous whistle. How to curl her hair with the wind instead of a damaging hot iron. How to sip whiskey in front of her friend without twisting her lips. She turns on the television, because it's time to take a break. The first commercial is for an electric kettle. *By God*, she says. The second commercial is for a hair curling cream. *Good lord*, she says. The third commercial is for assisted suicide. *Well that's a way*, she says. The sitcom she was anticipating comes on. "Men don't know how good they got it," a character says. She whips her hair and adjusts her bra so her breasts look pert. "Hell yeah!" another character responds. Canned cheers and laughter spill, soaking the set. A man walks on screen, seemingly tired from work. "Women don't know how good they got it!" he says. An even bigger can of laughter and cheers is opened. *Oh, I really do miss the commercials*, the woman says, and she goes back to her little projects.

Stephen Hawking & Robotic Dolls

Sometimes I think about those weird dolls that came out in the 90s that ate plastic fries and vegetable sticks, like they wanted to be real babies but couldn't manage it, and would choke on fingers of children, would suck a child's hair into the cold machinery of their heads leading to injuries that ended up on the news. I would see the videos of Stephen Hawking warning about artificial intelligence through his artificial voice, and you may laugh, saying, *He wasn't talking about dolls with moving mouths*, but I think normalizing these things is where the seed begins to sprout, where we think,

sure, robots can pretend to eat, that's fine,

and

yeah, they can be attached to paralyzed body parts to help the disabled function, it's only right,

and

well obviously the military should be able to benefit from new technology, we don't want them fighting with bows and arrows.

When life-like skin was developed for sex dolls, and robotic bees were invented to replace the ones we killed, there have been various points where we felt a pinch of nausea, whether we admitted it or not (and we probably didn't). I think we probably should have said something when the dolls started eating plastic fries and vegetable sticks and sucking children's hair into the cold machinery of their heads.

Bread Box

It's been a while since I've had a novel thought
that filled my limbs with a fleshy pink feeling.

Something honest, like the damp insides of our skin.
There's no lies there. No snakes.

If we were to shed our skin and use it to paper walls,
we'd have a nice place to gather and write a new
constitution,

to suck some red tea past agreeable lips
and indulge in sincere conversation

as though it were peanuty fudge.
But it's not the job for me specifically,

or my skin specifically.
Maybe for an old grandmother with faint

perfume and a second-hand onyx ring,
with fingers that gently move towards scrabble tiles,

placing them on the board in a kind confidence.
I mean, that's the kind of person we need

making our laws (don't quote me).
But me, I shake like the feathers of a startled bird

when the neighbors ask how I am.
So what good am I.

I'm just waiting for the pink to come along,
to slowly become visible,

like a flock of patient clouds at 6:30 in the morning,
and to, for once, not be terrified of when it will dissolve

into a dark black nothing
like the back corner of an empty bread box.

Contemplating More Vanilla Pudding or a Slightly Later Death

People revere animals for their ability to endure
the painfulness of the outdoors or of captivity.

"And they never complain!" They say.
"We don't deserve dogs!" They say this, too.

But I spend more time wondering how the elderly survive
neglectful senior homes, waiting for the volunteer

to come play checkers, their hands more youthful,
their fingers more flexible, their dumb eyes full

of pity and misplaced love.
The old man, his leg limp and strange like a dog

hit by a car, stares out the window, contemplating
more vanilla pudding or a slightly later death.

And he never complains.
My grandpa once said, "most people are good."

and I laughed toxic waves. But now, I think he was right.
In my early twenties, I stole some blue shirts

so I had something to wear at my Wal-Mart job.
The Loss Prevention Associate begged me for a reason

to not call the cops, and I told him I had no reason.
People revere animals for their ability to endure.

Tell me how we are not the same.

Please Show me That Someone Else Wanted Something and Never Received it

I felt really out of place during my one year of community college. It wasn't a self-esteem thing. Sometimes a girl would sneak a slender tube from her backpack and smack a translucent pink glaze on her lips, and the professor would look to me for an answer to a question I barely heard because I was thinking about how I was a person sitting in a small chair, in a large brick box, in an even larger planet, and how the aliens aren't going to see the translucent pink on the girl's lips, so why bother? If we really believe the aliens are so advanced and can end us all then let's work towards impressing them, maybe? Anyway, I couldn't say that to the professor, so I'd make something up, starting with "I think that…" and ending with "…But I don't know." So maybe it was a self-esteem thing after all. I lived down the street from the school and I could feel the wind from the other students as they walked past me on the sidewalk powered by some shiny hope smeared on the limbs of their life as if by a reckless child playing with glitter glue. But let's face it. They were powered by their parents paying their tuition, not by some sticky simile. So many years have passed since then. And I realize there is no irony in the fact that we describe the gone years in the same way that we indicate one has died. *Passed.*

Not only are those years dead, but they are unopened, like envelopes and packages thrown in the woods by an overwhelmed delivery person. When I drive by the trees along the highway, I look for them. *Please show me that someone else wanted something and never received it.* I realize how terrible this is, and I'm sure the bright, wide eyes of society's new young adults would shred my selfishness with each blink. Now sometimes when I pat some beet red color on my lips, I wonder who I am doing it for, and who is watching, and why I no longer care that I am a person sitting in a small chair, in a large brick box, in an even larger planet.

Boots Abandoned

not because they have grown

too small

but because we were supposed to

grow into them

and have only shrunken

into ourselves

like burning, plastic bells

The Entire World

Our white teeth have been knocked out of the sky

and all the world is forced to eat with raw gums.

And yet, people continue dancing with guns,

worshipping the cursive proclamations of skeletons.

Here, a mother's face crumbles into a sprawling pile

and her bed sheets are left in a sweaty clump.

There, a father's food tastes like the punctures

of cold wind through a thin winter coat.

Everywhere, we scream at the sky, the birds flying

calmly through it, the blue bright as a pearl.

Somewhere, a young man grins as he cleans his gun,

his silly hobby more important than the entire world.

Scarier Than Hell Ever Was

He's getting older now. Time to kill the weeds. Seal the driveway. Have the boys from down the street tear up the roof and slap on some fresh hot tar and sparkly new shingles. Time to hear their footsteps come through the ceiling as he waits in the kitchen, the living room, all the rooms. All the rooms that we call rooms but are actually just storage. Time to feel suffocated by the fact that all of the civilized world is storage. That the air takes turns with his lungs to store pollution. That his cells take turns storing cancer from talc powder and Mercury from tuna fish. Time to start imagining the metaphorical smell of burning flesh. To wonder if burning alive from climate change is scarier than hell ever was. Time to stop driving. Time to take the bus because the pollution is too heavy to carry. It's so unwieldy in its borderline intangibleness, its weight engulfing the grey folds of his brain like a grandfather's whiskey.

People Always "Used to" be Something

It's evident that telling a clever anecdote at a party should be my goal. I could be like a... what do you call it? A person. But I sit tightly and shyly and fail to say nonsense for the sake of speaking, things like "your wallpaper has an interesting texture," and "was it once paisley before cigarette smoke hid it with a disgusting brown film?" Anything to conversate and make others feel wanted.

But I do try, sometimes. I share that people once would have pun battles with guns and horses, and everyone responds with some alienating comment like, "oh, we only consider the past when it benefits us — let's take a look at this recipe speculated as used at the Last Supper and we can admire the idea of gods, the idea of children, the idea of inflatable whales in above ground pools, and all that middle class nonsense, because that's what we really want," and I sheepishly nod and go back to staring at the frizzy, once paisley wallpaper.

"I used to be a naturalist," says one partier, "I was curious like that writer who would cut open toothpaste tubes as a child because they couldn't sleep without knowing what the insides looked like," and the others' mouths fall agape so I can see the ginger snap crumbs on their white and pink tongues, and it reminds me of how my ex used to say people always "used to" be something;

they "used to" be a chef, they "used to" be on a show, they "used to" get really hot girls, but now they are just a dishwasher with a fleshlight and a lot of things they used to be. And I would like, for once, to just be something that I will someday no longer be, even if it's as small as being a person who can tell an amusing anecdote at a party that no one will remember.

Memoriam for the Grocery

A close up of my hand testing an avocado for ripeness.

A woman taking a box of laxative tea from the shelf,
looking at it, then putting it back, then ultimately picking it
up again, and wishing she hadn't.

The clanging sound of a kid smashing a cart up and down,
when he's too old to be smashing a cart up and down, and
is actually learning-about-condoms age.

A man looking at my chest, then my face with a half-smile,
then pretending to look at something nearby.

Kale chips, probably.

And you know this man doesn't eat kale chips.

Two preteen girls glancing at me, and one of them saying
"Why would someone wear that," as the other holds a hand
over her smirking mouth.

A woman with a thin scarf covering her white hair, using
her cart as a stabilizer, slowly tossing coupons onto the

conveyor belt, and being surprised as the conveyor belt turns on and the coupons start running away.

And then back to me, testing an avocado for ripeness, testing another avocado, testing the same avocado I tested previously, and then opting out of taking a gamble on these fruits(?) altogether.

The Electric City

Daytime in the electric city scatters a series of old decrepit men across each hour. Flecks of decay gather in their teeth; the odor of perceived laziness, the perfume of over-priced American dentistry. "I just need bread and milk." A woman says. "Bread and milk," She repeats while shaking her leather purse. But does she just need bread and milk? We wonder, and we keep our tiny bit of cash to ourselves. My first apartment was here right next to The Van Dyck; live music reverberated through our brown-stained windows, and old bodies danced in sequined skirts as though their frail feet could stomp hard enough to scare the tired ghosts from our efficiency apartments, the ghosts of our childhood hopes, all dead as a container of moldy strawberries. The boy I dated still performs at the bars and he doesn't have a car or health insurance, and he's losing his long black hair. It makes me want to hijack the sign at the Bowtie theatre and write "we're not lazy, we're just tired." I've tried talking to people about this. I've tried befriending the locals on social media, but it's a hellscape of "boss babes" supporting pyramid schemes, "bros" writing e-books about how to become a millionaire, and "Karens" not understanding the world has changed (including the job market). So I simply talk to myself through poetry that dwells on the negatives, and everyone calls it beautiful, because the prettiest thing they've seen lately is a pothole finally being filled, and a sparrow hopping along, pecking at greasy crumbs, filling his daytime in the electric city.

The New Yorker

I submitted some of my poems to The New Yorker. I must like pain. When I was a child, I would thread needles through tissue-thin layers of my skin and marvel at my minor injuries, my new little baggies of flesh that hung from my fingertips. Not much has changed, I see, as I stare at my rejection letters with a similar gross curiosity. I'm not thinking about it too-too much, I tell myself. I'm rubbing my fingers together over where they were once scarred from sewing needles that ate my body like metal termites. I suppose my skin went "back to normal," but I have no clear memory of what that normal was and who knows if normal is ever inherently good anyway. I'm tired of trying to figure things like that out. We all once had fun with philosophy and then it cracked and shriveled, like a house plant without a window. I own a book on walking through these kinds of forests that don't have paths. Forests as dark as the insides of our organs. It has something to do with a metaphorical trailblazing and I'm over it. I am struggling to turn its pages with my fingers; they are tapping on the armrest. I am impatiently waiting to receive my rejection from The New Yorker.

Our fig tree grows as though the world doesn't care what ugly is

as though an elderly woman doesn't still darken
her lash line with a broken kohl stick

and carefully fluff her thinning hair for company.

The grey branches are bent like car accidents
no one slowed to see,

and the fruit is hard as metal.
I too could grow when unable to see wanting mouths,

when the weeks ahead lay like empty sugar bags
and the months like an old molasses jar.

But instead, I wait for the mirror to carefully bend in a way
that reflects the fig tree through the window

like I'm not even there,
because that is how I could I feel holy.

Holy like a wren balancing at the top of a fruit,
its taupe cheeks round vessels pushing out ecstatic song

with lyrics like, "I am here! And yet, I am unobserved!"
Holy like an elderly woman, breaking her kohl stick,

saying "I won't use this goddamn thing anymore,"
and then using the broken pieces again the next day.

Part III:

Koinophobia

I Don't Know Why Butterflies are Considered Beautiful

My ex-boyfriend kept a butterfly wing in a tea tin.
Yes, a whole wing.

I wonder how odd it would be
to store a whole arm, or a whole leg, or a whole claw.

Then I remember we already do such things.
They're in Styrofoam and plastic containers

in the meat section of every grocery store,
or sometimes in cans in one of the aisles,

packed with preservatives, tasting of factories.
I don't know why butterflies are considered beautiful

(but of course they are).
Even if they are the brown of a dirty pan,

we say *look at those colors*,
which is the loving way in which a man perceives a woman

before he becomes bored.
I wait for the black feet of a butterfly to land on my nose

and to fascinate me, to fascinate me so deeply
that I am worse off when I become bored of it,

worse off than never having seen such a thing.
Perhaps so poorly off that after it died

I'd remove its wing and throw it into a tin I never open.
A tin I never open that will be discovered someday by a
lover

A lover someday who will not write a poem,
but will simply close the tin and forget.

The Trouble with Writing About Caterpillars

I pray for something not too cliché. Let's not say something that boils down to "they transform into something beautiful and flightful and so can you!" because that would be so disappointing that I would stop reading for weeks. Let's not kid ourselves. We are not growing wings. We must come to terms with the boundaries of being human. From birth to death, we are reading and rereading the book of "How Not to Succumb to Starvation" and/or the book of "How Not to Succumb to Mediocrity." Maybe the caterpillars would state "we never said losing our caterpillar bodies was worth being able to fly. Not everyone wishes to fly with fragile wings." Perhaps they would state, "death is the only mode of transformation." Or do caterpillars not speak in such clichés? Don't let me do this to them or myself. I really want to know how caterpillars feel about the whole butterfly thing.

Koinophobia

Three AWP panelists sat at a long rectangular table. One smiled. One didn't. One had an indecipherable mouth shape. Indecipherable Mouth Shape had his accomplishments listed off. Literary fiction award this, prestigious award that. Silence enveloped the seated guests. The woman next to me brushed lint from her green skirt. The man behind me muffled a cough. I adjusted my purse on my lap, though it was sitting just fine to begin with.

"And, their latest work, with an unmemorable title, will be adapted into a film."

A film?

Deafening applause rocked the room, and sharp shrieks of unmatched approval and envy erupted from the audience. The man who was muffling his cough was now wiping tears of joy from his cheeks. The woman in the green skirt removed her panties and showed the audience its wetness. Indecipherable Mouth Shape got on top of the rectangular table and pink and green spotlights shone on him as the rest of the room went dark. He strutted down the long table and stomped on the hands of the other panelists as they thanked him profusely. I continued to adjust my purse, to the left of my lap, to the right.

A fiiiiilmmmm! an announcer screamed.

"That's all we could ever dream of," a young woman whispered with shaking hands.

"This man has found to the key to not succumbing to mediocrity," a child said, and climbed up a towering stack of books and prayed at the top for an achievement even half as godly.

I opened my purse and looked for a crossword puzzle to distract me from the inexplicable chaos. The green light filled the inside of my purse, and people bumped into my seated body as they danced and danced to a song I couldn't hear.

Across
17. The fear of living an ordinary life.
11 letters.

"Okay, okay," said the announcer, "back to talking about... *books.*"

The florescent lights flickered back on and everyone seated themselves. I looked around and saw instantly bored and pale faces. The woman in the green skirt, panties drying, gave out an agitated sigh.

A Whale is Not the Biggest Thing in the Sea

The water is.
We forget the value of a human

comes down to the integrity of its society.
It is tempting to want to belong to the sea,

firstly because we cannot,
secondly because others can

 (the cuttlefish, the clownfish, the clams…)
Let us acknowledge that we grew these legs

for reasons. Look at them, in all their glory!
They even bend!

Imagine admiring the sun
from beneath the water;

it would run and blur like my mother
said the world did

before she had glasses
(though, she did say Christmas lights

were more beautiful then).
All the same, though, let's not aspire too hard

for any specific mindset. It's so limiting
to have goals.

We tell all the children, write them down,
display them in chalk on the road.

We say "big, bigger, big like a whole whale!"
and we watch them draw with blue chalk

a soft, lumpy animal.
A soft, lumpy animal, that yes, is big,

but the blank space around it is far larger,
and, I think, much more notable.

The Sea is for the Loved

Because it is too laborious
for an unloved person to tolerate horror

like that of a sea's great, dark blue expanse
with waves that fumble

like giant children
and octopuses, slimy but sharp

as sunlight,
probably sharper than us

startling bone-filled things
when we're incapacitated by small,

bright screens
or something as mundane as light

sparkling on water
and when we say things like "all's well

that ends well"
when we never reach the end

to know.

As Though Their Stiff Veins
Could Solve the Bird's Pain

A bird's blood-lined eye
pointed to the world
like the lost fingers
of arthritic hands.
I looked in the ball,
soil black, as though
expecting something.
An answer. A question.
I held its stunned form,
its stunning machine,
its feathers like mothers,
as it told me things.
Things like, "I am helpless
like a woman
told old fashioned lies,
helpless like a man
told none."
I drew a circle around it
to signal to predators,
"I resign"
as the bird's friends watched
with indifference.

Leaves snuck up to me,
the wind telling them what to do,
telling them what they had seen,
as though their stiff veins
could solve the bird's pain,
as though they could speak
with their browning limbs.

Orange Belly

Outside our window, we had an orange-bellied
Trogon — a magnificent green and orange bird —
 keep returning its plump body to the same branch
to observe our darkened naked bodies at night,
our sunscreen-soaked limbs at day, and its black
eyeball swallowed us in a fascination we didn't deserve
as would chocolate cake or pornography.

No one has a right to this pleasure, I thought.
We had been squinting into thick patches of leaves
for five hours, trying to find this feathered fellow,
only to open the door of our Airbnb
and have the beginning of this poem happen.
I wouldn't exactly say he was mocking us,
but you know, he looked like that kind of guy.

At Night

I had a round, wooden keepsake box in which I'd smudge

out my cigarettes

and if they weren't burned quite down to the filter

I'd retrieve it them from the ash

and smoke them again

This way I'd have something left to calm me

when there were men outside

my bedroom window like hummingbirds that think

everything pretty is a flower

The Word "Intolerable"

A boy told me he likes the taste of mold
because it tells him he's eating something
he shouldn't be.

To say something is useless is an insult to yourself.
It means "I am unable to come up with a use."

Maybe.

To say something is incomprehensible just means it is
incomprehensible to you.

I chew the end of my pen. It takes the imprints
of my teeth like a concerned dentist.

I cross out the lines.

To say something is worthless is to say that you are
unable to give it worth.

Is that true?

My little yellow bird flies to me. Everyone loves her
despite the sharp pinches of her beak.

I look at the teeth marks at the end of my pen.

To say something is intolerable... does that suggest a weak
ability to tolerate or a strong need for self-preservation?

My little yellow bird continues to bite me.
It reminds me I'm tolerating something I shouldn't be.

A Home to Virtually Nothing

Weeds are only ugly because they are plentiful.
I guess you could say they're like anything else.

There's some that grow in our city with dainty
purple flowers. I personally let them grow.

They're woven in between the messy brickwork
aside the driveway and they creep through

the middle of my yard like a violet stream.
I refuse to believe they're not beautiful

I'm stubborn. The woman across the street
sits on her lawn at night with a flashlight held

in her mouth, using both hands to pull these weeds.
What nonsense it feels like. I hate to break it to you,

but grass really isn't all that beautiful
and it makes your toes itch when it's wet

and you walk through it in sandals.
Also it's a home to virtually nothing and I've learned

that it originated as a display of wealth.
I recently decided, if we must have a tedious task

to propel us into adulthood, I would count the petals
on the purple flowers, touching each one,

as though counting them would make them live longer
because they would know that they were known.

Sonder

A bird's piece of down, like fraying lace, falls

A snowflake in the summer

And we say *Look, it is fragile*

Like our considerations of the universe

Look

It is so light that it flies away

When we try to catch it,

Like when we try to understand

Every passing human

as a life as vivid as ours

What's that word that means this, again?

Sonder.

Oh how we find these words fascinating,

As if every English word isn't just as complex

And the bird's piece of down

lands between a few blades of grass.

Mountains of Bones

The little blue flowers on the porch are dying,
lacking my care, sure, but also it's just the end

of their season. I wonder, is this what it's like
to be human? To shrivel, to wilt, wordlessly...

No, I remember, we will shout until the sweet
end. Until mountains of bones are excavated

by screaming wind or brilliant extraterrestrials.
And native flowers will rebloom, without memory

of when spring was once an excuse to write
cheerful poetry, and, perhaps for the first time,

it will be the song of rebirth. But for now, I will clip
these struggling flowers and close them into a book

for me to look back on happily, someday, as a time
when our horrible future was still "the future,"

a time when we choked out, "there's still time,"
like a child with a bone in his throat, turning blue.

Sympathy for Indoor Plants

They're not feeling their petals fumble in the rain-filled wind

(nor are they mourning a nearby dead chickadee. Their leaves curl at the edges like a cigarette end their pollen-filled eyes hardened like concrete).

I describe their wilting as inexplicable, but it should be obvious why it happens

(They live in the cold clay of factory-produced pots, their roots buried in soil that requires the slow blinking of clouds, the glittery invitations of the sun, the company of fresh rot).

Their silent whining crawls leglessly around the house

(making me think, "I'm not sure why I feel sad right now," making my lungs sigh with the air they clean, with my breath they make crisp like an envelope' sharp crease).

Destroying a Flower

It's funny, we see fleetingness as sad
as though it would be good if everything lasted forever,

giving us enough time to get sick of everything.
I prefer the heavy blue of temporary pleasures,

the strange aftertaste of gift-receiving,
When I was a kid,

I played the "he loves me, he loves not" game
with a little flower from the backyard.

It wasn't nearly as entertaining or fulfilling
as stories make it out to be.

I did not enjoy destroying a flower.
I'd rather allow the next passerby bee

to enjoy its colors
for a fleeting moment,

and maybe I could even see it again the next day,
but not the day after that.

How to Monetize Despair

I've read that the light at the end of the tunnel shrieks
as it closes, like a monkey with an infected tooth.

I'm not sure.

When I entered my mother's bedroom for the last time,
it smelled like no one had died.

Like not a single string of breath was torn
from the decorative bird cages and the potpourri pots.

Maybe that's why we sold all of her belongings
like they were just some shit we had lying around.

Maybe that's why my grandmother brought a raspberry
cheese pastry as though I could just go on eating.

I wondered if all deaths lead to a yard sale
if every corpse prompts a daughter to sit in the driveway

under the August sun, holding her mother's necklaces.

A woman said, "alls yall's stuff is overpriced."
She handed me a dollar in change for a brown dress.

I counted the coins by pushing them into my palm
the silver circles sinking into my hot skin,

and the borrowed cash drawer shrieked as it closed,
sealing the tunnel to what was and all it was worth.

A Less Brilliant Yellow

The house is heavy enough with lack of persons to crush bones into white pollen. I will soon resume begging coffee and alcohol and sleep to take care of my problems like they are a school nurse with too many sick children.

But for now, after showering, I will sit on the tub's cold edge with my towel, a deflated, overwhelmed snake wrapped languidly around my body, and I will wonder if anyone will come wrap their arms around me in similar fashion.

We could then shed our skins like lemons. Yes, like lemons, where what is underneath is even less sweet and a less brilliant yellow.

Why does it matter, to be held? I will ask this, and I will then try to refill the holes burrowed into my thoughts by worms preaching existential nihilism.

Nihilism has merit, sure, but it is unproductive, and I've come to value productivity over merit. If I must defend myself, please answer me what great accomplishment has been made in the name of "nothing matters," aside from the creation of books about how nothing matters.

In this moment, with those worms now dried flat like after rain, I will consider that the comfort of being held stems from assumptions, assumptions like, "this person loves me." and I will know that my life cannot be improved by mere assumptions.

We are Nothing if not Endless Seekers of the Beautiful

This is why when I write about my mother's death

and the things I have yet to confess,

it comes out as caterpillars and lemons and dandelions.

Trauma can be a magnifying glass for the blue petals of flowers,

the red peel of grape.

But I do wonder sometimes if I hold the glass too closely

when the sun is out.

I wonder if I'm just burning a hole right through.

About the Author

Lisa Mottolo is…

About Unsolicited Press

Unsolicited Press is based out of Portland, Oregon and focuses on the works of the unsung and underrepresented. As a womxn-owned, all-volunteer small publisher that doesn't worry about profits as much as championing exceptional literature, we have the privilege of partnering with authors skirting the fringes of the lit world. We've worked with emerging and award-winning authors such as Shann Ray, Amy Shimshon-Santo, Brook Bhagat, Kris Amos, and John W. Bateman.

Learn more at unsolicitedpress.com. Find us on twitter and instagram.